BRIDGES TO CHANGE

How Kids Live on a
South Carolina Sea Island

A WORLD OF MY OWN

BRIDGES TO CHANGE

How Kids Live on a South Carolina Sea Island

BY Kathleen Krull

PHOTOGRAPHS BY David Hautzig

Lodestar Books

DUTTON   NEW YORK

FRONTISPIECE: African hats on display at a Gullah festival

Library of Congress Cataloging-in-Publication Data
Krull, Kathleen.
Bridges to change: how kids live on a South Carolina Sea Island/by Kathleen Krull;
photographs by David Hautzig.—1st ed.
p.   cm.   (A World of my own)
"Lodestar books."
Includes index.
ISBN 0-525-67441-1
1. Gullahs—South Carolina—St. Helena Island—Social life and customs—
Juvenile literature.   2. St. Helena Island (S.C.)—Social life and customs—Juvenile
literature.   [1. Gullahs.   2. St. Helena Island (S.C.)—Social life and customs.]
I. Hautzig, David, ill.   II. Title.   III. Series: Krull, Kathleen. World of my own.
F277.B3K78   1995
975.7'99—dc20   93-42392   CIP   AC

Published in the United States by Lodestar Books,
an affiliate of Dutton Children's Books,
a division of Penguin Books USA Inc.,
375 Hudson Street, New York, New York 10014

Published simultaneously in Canada
by McClelland & Stewart, Toronto

Editor: Virginia Buckley   Designer: Joseph Rutt
Map by Matthew Bergman

Printed in Hong Kong   First Edition   10 9 8 7 6 5 4 3 2 1

to Virginia Buckley, for being there

—K. K.

To be a successful photographer, you need a keen eye,
the right equipment . . . and a little help. Thanks to Randy Cole,
Mike Luppino, Doug Nobiletti and the gang at MyLab, Skip and
the gang at WestSide Camera, Beverly Adler, and Derek Price.

—D. H.

Acknowledgments

The author gratefully acknowledges the participation of Travis Johnson and Martha Chisholm and their families, as well as the help of Emory Campbell and Walter Mack of the Penn Center of the Sea Islands. Also helpful were Julie Dash and her film *Daughters of the Dust;* Dr. Laverne Davis of St. Helena Elementary School; Harriet Cochran and Donald West of the Avery Research Center, College of Charleston; Mary Horschke; Linda and Rodney Westbury; Dolly Oliver of Carver-Edisto Middle School; Anne Brown of Jane Edwards Elementary School on Edisto Island; Marian Knott of Bed, No Breakfast; Jery B. Taylor; Sheila and Michael Cole; the Frogmore Hotel and the Shrimp Shack; and most of all, Paul Brewer. Special thanks to Jennifer Lyons, Michele Rubin, and especially Susan Cohen, of Writers House.

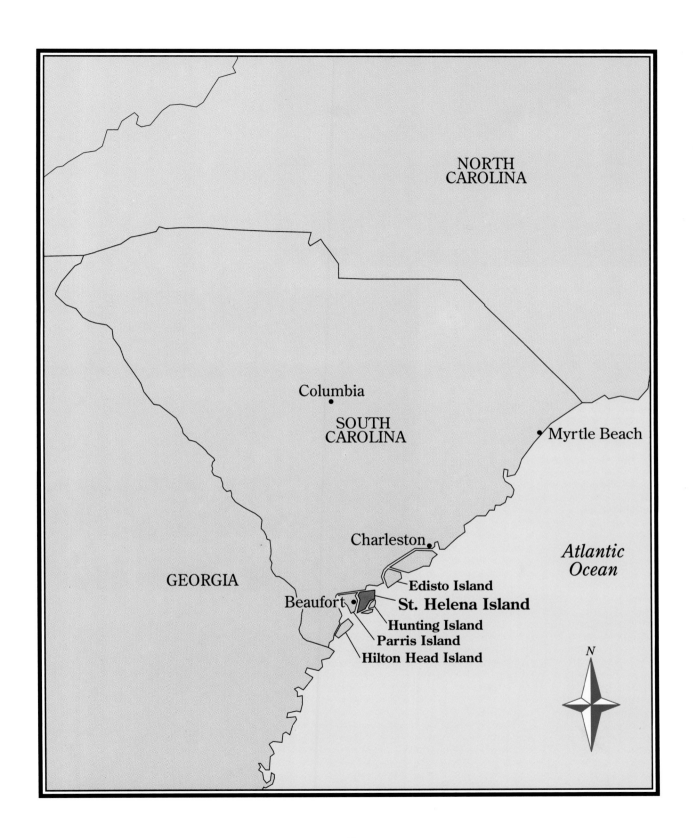

NORTH
CAROLINA

Columbia
•

SOUTH
CAROLINA

• Myrtle Beach

Charleston
•

Atlantic
Ocean

Edisto Island

GEORGIA

St. Helena Island

Beaufort •

Hunting Island
Parris Island

Hilton Head Island

N

LEFT: Alligators occasionally appear in surrounding creeks.

RIGHT: Travis Johnson's yard has the best trees for climbing (BELOW) and it also provides berries and other good things to eat.

One day, ten-year-old Travis Johnson discovered five new puppies romping right in his own yard. They are just one of the surprises found in his giant backyard on St. Helena Island in South Carolina.

Travis's corner of the island is full of the unexpected, like the alligator in the creek, the one big enough to be the parent of the babies he saw in the nearby marsh. His yard keeps him active climbing the huge oak tree, with the branches his mother named after the fifty states when she was a child. It even supplies food. "If we don't go to the store we can go crabbing in the creek," says Travis. Peach, pear, and plum trees thrive. Each one of his relatives' houses has chickens and a little garden with okra, tomatoes, watermelon, and corn. Even a wild plant called sour sally, which grows around his mobile home, is good for munching. "You suck the sugar out."

Although big chunks of Travis's African family history are missing and can never be traced, he knows that in America his family has lived on this property since the days of slavery. Travis has heard about the way slave-owners broke up families. His own great-grandmother was separated from her husband and given to someone else; her husband had to take a new partner. "When you were a slave," Travis's mother tells him, "you had no choice."

Across St. Helena Island, Martha Chisholm, age ten, also has a huge backyard. Its ten acres are more than enough space for riding her bike, jumping rope, and playing with her cousins, who live here, too.

Martha's roots on this land go deep—she is the ninth generation of her family to live amid the beautiful seascape of St. Helena Island. Her family is part of the island's long, rich history. Her great-great-great-grandfather, an enslaved African freed after the Civil War, was the one who bought the land where she lives.

Martha Chisholm plays with a cousin in her yard.

The main thing Martha has learned about slavery is that "if slaves tried to get away they would be caught no matter what. You could not get away." Martha's ancestors in Africa, an aunt has told her, were kings and queens. Captured and forced to sail to the United States in the holds of ships, these ancestors became slaves on the plantations of wealthy whites, where not only their African titles but even their names were forbidden. The men in Martha's family, for example, have different last names because they had different owners. Martha has a simple reason for making Abraham Lincoln's birthday her favorite holiday after Christmas and Thanksgiving: "Because he freed the slaves."

St. Helena, where Travis and Martha live, is one of the Sea Islands off the coast of South Carolina and Georgia. The islands were once one of the most remote areas of the United States. Until this century, the only way to reach them was by boat. There were no bridges to St. Helena until the Depression, and some islands still don't have any.

Until bridges were built, the ocean kept St. Helena Island remote.

Where Is St. Helena?

Extending along a 250-mile stretch of southern coast, there are hundreds of Sea Islands, perhaps thousands. St. Helena Island is halfway between Charleston, South Carolina, and Savannah, Georgia. Formerly known as Frogmore, from an eighteenth-century plantation of the same name, the island covers fifteen square miles.

During the Civil War, northern forces occupied the Sea Islands early on and freed the slaves. White plantation owners fled, and General William Sherman ordered that the plantations be divided up and given to the former slaves. After the war, some plantation owners ignored the order and returned to the land. But many freed slaves held onto their property or were even able to buy more, leaving it to their heirs. The parcels that the extended families in St. Helena live on are known as heirs property. Anyone related to the family has the right to live there.

For many years, islanders had a self-sufficient life—casting nets for crab, shrimp, fish, and oysters; hunting deer, rabbits, raccoons, ducks, and other game; growing crops; making quilts and baskets. Midwives delivered babies, and people practiced folk medicine. Then bridges came, and with them change.

Islanders have traditionally grown their own crops, such as these onions.

African-Americans in South Carolina

As many as two-thirds of the ancestors of American blacks entered this country through the port of Charleston, South Carolina. By 1860, this state had more enslaved Africans than any other state, some four hundred thousand. The Africans brought valuable skills with them that enriched slave-owners, leading to a gulf between the enormously wealthy and the impoverished. They built the plantations, cultivated rice, herded cattle (the word cowboy *may have originated on the South Carolina coast, to describe adult men who tended cattle), fished, practiced medicine, and grew high-quality cotton, which made huge profits for the plantation owners.*

Nearly every Sea Island has a legend about a group of Africans captured from the Ibo tribe. It is said that when their boat landed, the Ibos stepped on shore in their chains, realized what was in store for them, turned around, and began walking home, chanting, "The water brought us, the water will take us away." Weighted down by their chains and in front of their horrified captors, the Ibos— men, women, and children—chose drowning rather than a life of captivity.

Africans were brought to this country against their will, and they were controlled with guns, chains, and whips. Because of the isolation of the Sea Islands,

they were brought here later than to any other area of the South, particularly after the slave trade became illegal in 1808. Thus, at the time the slaves were freed in 1865, many African-born people were living on the islands and shaped the culture.

Great disparity between rich and poor can be found in the Sea Islands.

Spanish moss grows on the trees, creating an atmosphere of mystery.

In this isolation and tranquility, it can seem, even today, as though time has stood still. The islands remain a haven for numerous plant and animal species. Ancient oak trees lean into the roads, forming arches. Sunlight filters through the Spanish moss overhanging the branches, spotlighting the pink and red azaleas. Purple wisteria vines climb over anything they can. Peering into the dense forests, one can imagine the days when Cherokee and other tribes were the first residents on the islands, and when pirates such as the notorious Blackbeard and others used lonely Carolina beaches as hiding places. People then may have heard the same kinds of birdcalls and smelled the same things—the perfumy scent of yellow jessamine, the sweetness of tall pines, the salty tang of the Atlantic Ocean—that Travis and Martha do today.

The roads where Travis and Martha and other children live have no names. Dirt lanes wander across creeks, around palmetto trees, or through marshes. People don't travel in residential areas after dark. Without streetlights, it is not easy to find the way. If someone does get lost and asks for directions, unless the person is known, he or she is not likely to get an answer. Families with roots that go back hundreds of years have a tradition of keeping to themselves; they are proud and protective. One sees all kinds of houses, though perhaps there are more trailer homes here than elsewhere—such homes are more convenient to get onto the islands. But sections of the islands are still undeveloped, giving an outsider the unusual sensation of being lost in time.

Away from the highway, roads are unpaved and unmarked.

Even the language of the Sea Islands is unique. Longtime residents speak Gullah (pronounced *GULL-a*)—a distinctive blend of English (possibly Elizabethan English) with words and grammatical rules from West African languages. *Gullah* is also the word used to describe people from the Sea Islands, or the rural African-American culture that exists here. Relatively little is known about the Gullah people. Visitors will rarely even hear the language; speakers switch to English when talking to outsiders. Because the people are separated from the mainland by marshes and swamps, their language and culture have not become Americanized as rapidly as those of other groups that have come to this country.

ABOVE: African culture can be found in everything from language to drumming.

RIGHT: Watery seascapes lie between St. Helena and the mainland.

The Gullah Language

The word Gullah *may have come from a shortened form of Angola, a West African country where many slaves were taken from, or from a Liberian group of tribes known as the Golas, who lived between Sierra Leone and the Ivory Coast.*

The Gullah language was developed during the slave trade, when communication created a crisis. Enslaved Africans were punished severely for being "uppity" if they spoke formal English. Slaves who did not speak English were even considered more desirable, because they were thought less capable of plotting rebellions. At the same time, their own African languages were outlawed.

Gullah first emerged as a secret language, a deliberate code that slaves, aliens in a hostile environment, could use among themselves. It was a language they could speak in common, a way to ease their loneliness and fear. Gullah is its own language; it is not "primitive English." But racist slave-owners thought it was, and used this as further justification for making Africans into slaves. Ironically, whites, who were vastly outnumbered by the slaves, began to pick up Gullah, too, especially as more and more white children were raised by Gullah-speaking women.

Some Gullah expressions are "ugly too much" (very ugly), "sweetmouth" (flatter), "long eye" (envy), "hot the water" (bring the water to a boil), "rest you mouth" (shut up), and "pakpakpak" (knock). If you want to say something is very small, you might say "small small." If the thing is really tiny, you might say "small, small, small."

But the bridges built in this century have brought change, and people are leaving the islands for jobs or education. Because of this dispersal, the mysterious, musical Gullah language is starting to disappear, fading with each passing generation.

Martha's grandmother, for example, used to speak Gullah fluently, but lost much of it when she moved to New York for a while. "Unless you hear it all the time, you lose it," she explains. Martha's mother can understand Gullah but she cannot speak it. Martha herself neither speaks nor understands Gullah.

Children are, in fact, discouraged from speaking Gullah, both by the schools and by many parents. The language is frequently thought of as the clumsy dialect of uneducated people.

"When kids leave here, talking like that doesn't help them," Travis's mother says. "You become a spectacle; people laugh at you." People who live off the islands are known to find Gullah backward, even a source of humor. They buy recordings of Gullah speech as comedy albums. City kids mock island kids for "talking bad."

So if Travis says something in Gullah, his mother jumps in with, "Uh-uh, say it the right way!" She feels that her children are picking up Gullah from some kids whose parents *don't* discourage them.

Travis's sister, Chantel, is more apt to use Gullah than he is, because she spends more time around her Gullah-speaking grandmother. At school, if Chantel says something in Gullah, "the teacher will correct me." This doesn't bother Chantel—she thinks that the teacher is right. If kids speak Gullah all the time, the school recommends speech class.

FACING PAGE: Today, bridges are bringing many changes.

"Teachers are stricter now than when we were growing up," says Travis's mother. "And children today talk better than we did. Gullah may be okay for joking around, but when you teach your children to want the best things out of life, you prepare them to speak like they're educated."

Travis at school with his teacher

Although the use of Gullah has decreased dramatically in the last forty or so years, the language has been finding more respect. Instead of being considered merely a careless version of English, Gullah is now recognized by scholars as a language in its own right, one worthy of study. Some feel that Gullah, far from being inferior, is valuable and should, in fact, be preserved before it becomes a dead language. People are becoming interested in learning it; in the city of Charleston, there are college courses that teach Gullah. Sea Islanders who grew up speaking it are beginning to take pride in the language, as part of their rich heritage. In general, many people have been increasingly unhappy with newspaper articles or books that ridicule their language and life-style.

Martha likes using the computer.

The country of Sierra Leone is believed to have influenced the Gullah culture.

Very recently, researchers have discovered connections between Gullah and the language of Sierra Leone, a country in West Africa. Some people now believe that, because of this and other similarities, many of the Africans brought here were from Sierra Leone. There is no way of proving such a connection, however, since records are few or nonexistent.

As in Sierra Leone, most people on the Sea Islands live in extended families, and they have done so for generations. Martha lives with her mom (a single mother), her grandmother, and her cousin Justin. Nearby live more relatives: "aunts and uncles, in-laws and outlaws, and cousins—lots, lots, lots." Grandparents are much-respected figures and are particularly important in children's lives, as the parents may have to travel to other areas for jobs. Every day, her grandmother fixes Martha's hair into one of three major styles. Martha doesn't have much say over which style—"no, no, no"—but she always likes her hair and never has a complaint.

Travis, whose parents are divorced (his father is in Chicago), lives with his mother, sister, aunt, and a dog named Spud—all surrounded by close relatives.

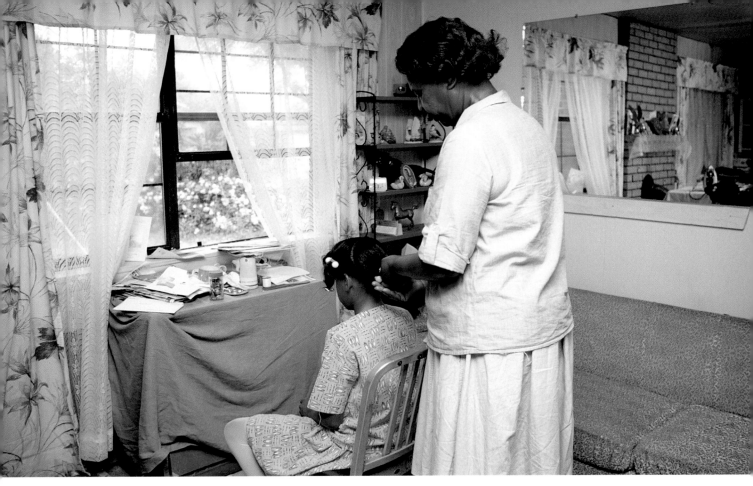

ABOVE: Martha's grandmother styles her hair.

LEFT: Travis plays with Spud in his yard.

African Ties

People from St. Helena who have visited Sierra Leone report numerous, almost uncanny similarities between the two areas. The two cultures share the same diet combinations of fish, rice, and produce; quilting and fishing net patterns; and styles of singing, dancing, and drumming. The similarities in language, including songs and expressions that the St. Helena people learned as children, are especially strong.

Besides their language, so unintelligible to outsiders, Gullahs are most famous in South Carolina for beautiful sweetgrass baskets. Basketmaking was one of the few ways slaves were allowed to acknowledge their African identity. The intricate techniques they used come from Sierra Leone and other countries in West Africa. Originally made for work such as winnowing rice and carrying infants, the baskets are now considered art, and are displayed in museums as contemporary examples of an ancient African craft. Some basket makers have become internationally known folk artists. Collectors value Gullah baskets and are willing to pay high prices for them. Today, as development degrades the environment and blocks public access to the marshes where the sweetgrass grows, the baskets will become scarcer and even more valuable.

A display of the popular Gullah baskets, made from the local sweetgrass

RIGHT: Martha enjoys singing hymns at church.

BELOW: Remains of a church built in 1740

BOTTOM: Travis attends church several times a week.

Religion has been important on the Sea Islands for centuries. Enslaved Africans were not permitted to gather together—the owners feared planned rebellion—unless it was for religious services. Churches have often been the educational and social centers of the communities.

Martha describes church as *"very important"* in her life. She attends services at one of various Baptist churches every Sunday, and enjoys special occasions, such as fundraisers or weddings. She likes singing hymns, her favorites being "I'll Fly Away" and "Wasn't That a Mighty Day When Jesus Christ Was Born." She especially likes serving as an usher, which she gets to do about once a month. Travis goes to the Kingdom Hall of Jehovah's Witnesses every Tuesday, Thursday, and Sunday, and sometimes has Bible study at home on Mondays.

Gullah Influences

Storytelling is a well-developed tradition on the Sea Islands. Most outsiders recognize the Uncle Remus stories, for example, which originated here. In these tales Brer Rabbit, the bold trickster, continually outwits his more powerful enemies, proving that intelligence wins the day over brute force. Collected from former slaves by a white journalist from Georgia, Joel Chandler Harris, the 263 Uncle Remus tales were published in eight volumes beginning in 1896. They have appeared in many forms and variations ever since.

The influence of Africans on American music has been immeasurable, and most people know at least one song that originated on the Sea Islands, "Michael, Row the Boat Ashore." In the days when the only transportation was small boats, each plantation had a boat crew with its own original work songs.

Michael may have been the lead oarsman of a particular boat, or the song may have double meanings about escape and release.

Gullahs have been active in community organizations that influenced Martin Luther King, Jr., and in turn, the history of the civil rights movement in the United States. The Penn Center in St. Helena, for example, was a meeting place for civil rights groups in the 1960s; the 1963 March on Washington, D.C., site of King's famous "I Have a Dream" speech was partly planned here.

The Sea Islands are renowned
for good storytellers.

Martha and Travis go to the Penn Center after school.

Martha and Travis both spend their after-school hours at the Penn Center, a community service organization that began as the first school in the South for freed slaves. At the center, the children complete their homework, go for nature walks or hunt for fiddler crabs, and learn about Gullah history and culture. Sometimes Martha and Travis board a creaky old blue bus that takes them strawberrypicking, for example.

Because of schoolwork, and her activities at the Penn Center, Martha's free time is very limited. Besides jumping double-dutch and riding into town to help her mother shop for household things, her favorite thing to do is watching the news. Her mother keeps the news on so Martha can become informed, but, says Martha, "My mother doesn't have to tell me to watch it because I think it's important." Her favorite show is *60 Minutes.* The issues that most interest her are the environment, health, and how people treat one another. She has strong opinions about events, even those that occur far from South Carolina. For example, she says about the trials of the Los Angeles policemen who beat Rodney King: "It's really sad what they did to him, but they were mad. I don't understand why they did it, or why the police officers stood and watched and didn't try to stop it."

Martha excels at jumping double-dutch.

Martha watches TV news while she eats dinner with her cousin.

In his free time, Travis plays basketball and baseball in the big park across the street from his school. At home, his mother is teaching him how to skip stones across the creek. He likes to draw and do lettering, and he has a thriving baseball card collection. Travis gets an allowance for doing chores, and he almost always saves it. Right now the money is going toward a mountain bike and a saxophone.

Skipping stones across Travis's creek

Travis enjoys basketball, baseball, and kickball.

Travis displays
his baseball card
collection.

Travis is saving
up for a new
mountain bike.

Although St. Helena has so much natural beauty, it has disadvantages, too, as the cinder blocks underneath most houses suggest. This is a flood zone, and the weather, especially during hurricane season, can be nasty. Martha was terrified one year when a storm forced her and her family to evacuate the island for a day. Her redbrick house wasn't damaged, but a trailer across the road was. "It got knocked down off its blocks and hasn't got back on its feet yet," she says. "Everything in there's still sideways for now!"

Travis, whose roof was damaged by another hurricane, occasionally has nightmares. "A hurricane will pick up my school and land it on Mars," he says.

Cinder blocks keep houses raised above the occasional flood waters.

Martha has learned not to let mosquitoes interfere with bike riding.

Good insect repellent and sturdy screens are musts on St. Helena Island, since mosquitoes and sand gnats can be annoying some nine months out of twelve. Outdoor work is best done in the early morning, before the bugs get bad. Martha handles the bug problem by staying indoors much of the time, particularly in the evenings. Travis, too, is indoors when the sun starts going down. When outdoors, Martha usually wears long pants and shirts with long sleeves. As for the combination of bugs and bike rides: "You have to keep your mouth shut."

For some, the pace of life on the Sea Islands is too slow. Jobs are scarce, particularly for those with education. The Marine training station on nearby Parris Island draws many people. Travis's mother was an operating-room technician in the military and now is a nurse at a local hospital. Martha's mother was a radio operator and currently works as a pharmacy clerk on another island.

Although many people don't have cars, public transportation is minimal. As a result, more people hitchhike here than in other parts of the country. The hitchhiking system operates through neighbors and family—hitchers don't take rides from just anyone. Black hitchhikers will not signal if white drivers approach, partly because they know from experience that whites won't stop, and partly because they like to be acquainted with whoever is picking them up. People have been reported missing or hurt while hitchhiking, and neither Travis nor Martha is allowed to get rides this way.

Recently St. Helena, like many other Sea Islands, has become attractive to outside developers. Parts of it are already commercialized; a five-lane highway that will cut across the entire island is now being planned. Many residents oppose the highway because they feel it is a step toward the kind of development that has transformed the nearby island of Hilton Head. Some longtime black residents think that such development comes at their expense, especially when fair prices are not always paid for their property. In 1950, for example, Hilton Head, the recent winter retreat for President Bill Clinton, was almost entirely black; now whites outnumber blacks by more than eight to one. Playgrounds for rich people—lavish resorts, golf courses, tennis clubs, spectacular private homes, marinas full of yachts—are displacing families who have lived there for generations.

FACING PAGE: Festivals are an opportunity to sell traditional wares.

Security guards keep outsiders from entering private property.

As developers move in, they buy up whole sections of land or build islands from swamps and then declare the areas private, which restricts access to the local population. Signs, guards, and gates now block admittance to land that used to be open for hunting, fishing, and playing. This has happened on all sides of St. Helena, and it strikes people like Martha's grandmother as "another form of slavery."

A sign of change that most directly affects people is outsiders who want to buy the land that has been in their families for many years. Such development means that property that was formerly worth little is now highly valuable. Outsiders have tried to get Martha's family to sell. Their answer is no. Among their reasons, they believe that other areas are not as safe for bringing up kids. Visitors are amazed at the children's extra freedom, that here they can play outside until eleven at night, as long as they wear insect repellent.

Travis's mother feels that if her children were growing up in a big city, where "you have to fight every day," they simply wouldn't survive. St. Helena, on the other hand, is comparatively free of crime, gangs, and drugs. A lot of people have tried to buy their property, but the Johnsons will never sell—even though, as the land rises in value, the taxes on it keep jumping without warning.

Sometimes, on the hottest days of the year, Travis visits Hunting Island State Park, the only beach on St. Helena still open to the public. All crunchy with shells, the beach is a paradise for nature lovers. Giant sea turtles, now all but extinct, lay eggs on this beach each spring.

The kids sometimes visit the only beach on St. Helena that is still open to the public.

Martha also makes trips to the beach. For summertime reading, she loves all kinds of books, from self-help guides (how to make better grades, how to do better in sports, what to do if you get in trouble) to stories (fairy tales, Gullah tales, creepy mysteries). She doesn't care if the kids in a book are black or white, "as long as it's a good book." Her taste in music includes rap, jazz, opera, and gospel.

Travis reads comic books and mysteries, and has been known to read scary Stephen King—much to his mother's disapproval. He likes religious music, rhythm and blues, and easy listening. He loves Kenny G so much that he can't wait to learn saxophone and play it in the school band.

FACING PAGE: Travis likes to draw.

BELOW: Travis plays the recorder at school and plans to learn saxophone.

Martha's favorite food is pizza, which she often gets at her favorite restaurant. But she also eats foods most American kids don't—oysters, shrimp, crab, conch, and clams, the local bounty. At home she usually eats beans and rice or macaroni and cheese. Travis's favorite food is pizza, too; he also likes shrimp. His uncle works on a shrimp boat, so Travis knows that when he eats shrimp it might be from his uncle's catch. Neither Martha nor Travis has ever had the local specialty, Frogmore stew (with shrimp, sausage, corn, and rice), also known as Low Country Boil.

ABOVE: Fishing is an important industry.

LEFT: Pizza is Martha's favorite food.

Martha and Travis are growing up in an almost all-black world. White children are by far the minority at their school. For the most part, Martha and Travis say, the kids in school get along fine, though sometimes they tease or wrestle one another. Martha feels that white kids get teased more at her school than blacks. She herself does not encounter discrimination in daily life. "I get treated the same way everyone else gets treated," she says. "And it doesn't make any difference to me that my teacher is Caucasian. She's nice, she teaches me, and she looks after the class very well."

Travis, on the other hand, *has* experienced discrimination. He has been in line at a store, with a white person behind him, when "the clerk will skip me and take the white person first." In St. Helena, younger blacks, especially males, are sometimes stopped by police. According to Travis's mother, a black male in a nice car is apt to get pulled over and asked for some identification and registration.

Travis wants to be a doctor when he grows up because, as he says, "You save a lot of lives." His mother, as a nurse, is an inspiration to him, and he also has an uncle who is a doctor in Florida. He hasn't decided whether he will stay in St. Helena. Texas sounds tempting, especially since he has cousins there.

FACING PAGE: Black and white kids
mingle at a Gullah festival.

ABOVE: Martha gets straight A's in school and thinks about becoming a lawyer.

Martha is thinking about being a lawyer. "You get a lot of money and a good education," she says. "You get to talk a lot; you get to speak with your clients." Her last report card contained straight A's. Thinking ahead, she hopes to get a scholarship to the University of South Carolina. As a lawyer, it wouldn't matter if her clients were black or white. "I'm not really interested in what color people are," she says. "I just want to win the case and help them get through the rough and tough times." One thing she is certain about is that, at this point, she has no plans to get married.

She's less sure about where she will live. It won't be New York ("too noisy"), but it could be Michigan. She hasn't actually been there yet, but her Michigan cousin visits every summer and tells her all about it. Or she might very well return to St. Helena after college. "I could help my family out and help the Penn Center raise money," she says, referring to the Penn's programs to help black families retain their land.

Wherever she lives when she grows up, she wants it to be a place with a lot of windows, so she has a view. And if it is in St. Helena, her windows will either look out over scenes of stunning natural beauty— or will reveal a landscape completely changed from the one of her childhood.

FACING PAGE: Future changes may affect the natural beauty of St. Helena Island.

For Further Reading

Dennis, Denise. *Black History for Beginners*. New York: Writers and
    Readers Publishing, 1984.

Hamilton, Virginia. *Many Thousand Gone: African Americans from
    Slavery to Freedom*. New York: Knopf, 1993.

Haskins, James. *Black Music in America: A History Through Its
    People*. New York: HarperCollins, 1987.

Lauture, Denize. *Father and Son*. New York: Philomel, 1992.

Lester, Julius. *The Tales of Uncle Remus: The Adventures of Brer
    Rabbit*. New York: Dial Books for Young Readers, 1987.
    Also *More Tales of Uncle Remus* (1988), *Further Tales of
    Uncle Remus* (1990), and *The Last Tales of Uncle Remus* (1994).

Lyons, Mary E., compiler. *Raw Head, Bloody Bones: African-American
    Tales of the Supernatural*. New York: Scribner, 1991.

Myers, Walter Dean. *Now Is Your Time: The African-American
    Struggle for Freedom*. New York: HarperCollins, 1991.

Westridge Young Writers Workshop. *Kids Explore America's
    African-American Heritage*. Santa Fe: John Muir Publications, 1993.

Index

Page numbers in *italics* refer to photographs and map.

About the Author

KATHLEEN KRULL'S recent books include three other volumes in the A World of My Own series, with photographer David Hautzig. She has also written *Lives of the Musicians,* a 1993 *Boston Globe-Horn Book* Honor Book in Nonfiction and a *Publishers Weekly* Best Book of 1993.

Ms. Krull loves interviewing, and when she isn't asking nosy questions, she writes book reviews for *L.A. Parent* and other magazines. She lives in San Diego with her husband and has been to the South several times to visit friends and relatives.

About the Photographer

DAVID HAUTZIG was born and raised in New York City. He graduated from Syracuse University in 1987 with a degree in broadcast journalism but turned to photography instead. Besides the A World of My Own series, he has photographed *On the Air: Behind the Scenes at a TV Newscast,* by Esther Hautzig, and written and photographed *DJ's, Ratings, and Hook Tapes.* He also works as a commercial interiors photographer. He still lives in New York City.